ZZZ WHILE MEN SLEEP

G. Janice Miller

ARPress

ILLUMINATING IDEAS.
EMPOWERING VOICES

ARPress
45 Dan Road Suite 5
Canton MA 02021

Hotline: 1(888) 821-0229
Fax: 1(508) 545-7580

Ordering Information:
Quantity sales. Special discounts are available on quantity purchases by corporations, associations, and others. For details, contact the publisher at the address above.

Printed in the United States of America.

ISBN-13:	Softcover	979-8-89389-373-1
	Hardcover	979-8-89389-374-8
	eBook	979-8-89389-372-4

Library of Congress Control Number: 2024916622

TABLE OF CONTENTS

INTRODUCTION

Because of the overwhelming number of products and services available in today's market we are doing more research prior to making purchases. Digital technology puts massive amounts of information at our fingertips, helping us become informed consumers. Alerts notify us when something is being misrepresented in advertisements so we can avoid being taken. How many times just this week have you queried the Internet prior to making a decision?

While Men Sleep is a concise five-day study about being an informed decision-maker regarding spiritual matters. Paul told Timothy in latter times some will depart from the faith because they are giving heed to deceiving spirits and doctrines of demons (1 Timothy 4:1). While the desire to be an alert, informed consumer of products and services is on the rise, we see the opposite trend when it comes to the spiritual. This results in many being deceived. Paul exhorted in Romans 13:11 to those who understand the present time, now is the time to awake out of sleep. While Men Sleep is dedicated to the watchmen among God's people (Ezekiel chapter 33) who sound the alarm in Zion.

God has given every human the power to make choices. *Now listen! Today I am giving you a choice between life and death, between prosperity and disaster* (Deuteronomy 30:15 NLT). Matthew records Jesus's' lesson about the choice between the narrow and wide gates. *Enter through the narrow gate, For wide is the gate and broad is the road that leads to destruction, and many enter through it. But small is the gate and narrow the road that leads to life, and only a few find it* (Matthew 7:13-14 NIV).

We must be alert against our enemy. He is an illusionist who puts up billboards along the way and paints deceitful pictures of how life is good on the broad road. This is false advertising. What he doesn't disclose is the broad road leads to destruction. Those who follow the road do so because they are drawn away by their own lust and believe a lie (II Thessalonians 2:7-12).

If we choose life on the narrow road, we seek to walk in unity with Christ daily. We live as Paul, *So I strive always to keep my conscience clear before God and man* (Acts 24:16 NIV). These who follow Christ have a bond with likeminded believers which supersedes organizational lines and cannot be understood by the human intellect. Walking in unity with Christ results in the greatest fulfillment a human can experience. Why choose any other way?

At the end of each session there is an opportunity for **Reflection and Prayerful Consideration** where you can identify the statements or scriptures that impacted you the most. Turn these into a prayer of response to God and allow Him to speak **Next Steps** into your heart and spirit.

All scriptures quoted in these sessions are from The Authorized (King James) Version unless otherwise noted.

Session One

The Dangers of Deception

Lucifer (aka Satan, the devil, the old serpent, the dragon) was the original drama queen. He drank his own concoction, believed his own lies, and somehow managed to convince a third of the angels in heaven that he should be equal to God and worshiped as God. That started a war, and here's what happened:

- *And there was war in heaven: Michael and his angels fought against the dragon; and the dragon fought and his angels, And prevailed not; neither was their place found any more in heaven. And the great dragon was cast out, that old serpent, called the Devil, and Satan, which deceiveth the whole world: he was cast out into the earth, and his angels were cast out with him* (Revelation 12:7–9).

When he and his angels were cast out, Satan went to and fro in the earth, weaving his web in preparation for God's special creation, man. It's like a spider that weaves its web, knowing that at some point an insect will fly or walk into it and become entangled. Satan specializes in sensationalism and setting up illusions. Sensationalism is the use of exciting or shocking stories or language at the expense of accuracy, to provoke public interest or excitement. A whole philosophy is developed around sensationalism, one fueled by Satan's ideas. It states that something is only good if it gratifies the senses, the flesh. This plan has helped Satan deceive multitudes over the centuries because it takes advantage of a couple things about human nature:

- Humans tend to gravitate to the sensational. We are attracted to elements that are bigger, better, brighter, higher, shinier, glitzy, glamorous, self-indulgent, and self-gratifying. We tend to easily fall into states of discontentment. Paul tells us the value of finding contentment in Philippians 4:11. He said he had learned that whatever situation he was in to be content. Learning to find contentment with what God provides for us is one of the greatest defenses we have against our enemy. As soon as we reveal signs of discontentment, we give Satan a clue about how to get to us.

- Humans tend *not* to turn over the rocks and examine things carefully to determine what is real or fake in the light of scripture. Some of us are very prone to take things at face value, on the surface.

As an illusionist, Satan paints beautiful pictures to entice prey. It's not until people are entangled that they realize the reality of it is not what was sold to them. It's similar to seeing a movie production with over-the-top visual effects and then finding out it was a very simple set that had very sophisticated illusions.

Why are we hearing so many warnings about deception? Deception has been around since the Garden of Eden, but based on what Paul shared with Timothy concerning our day, this generation must be on guard for a super-invasion (1 Timothy 4:1).

Paul told the Corinthians they were too easily falling for the deception of Satan II Corinthians 11:3). They had been fooled by sensationalism. Because signs and wonders accompanied aberrant teaching, they fell for it.

Satan's goal has remained the same throughout history: to be worshiped. His modus operandi is outlined in scripture. His project plan, titled "Deception," has two long poles:

1. Attempt to corrupt the Word of God.

2. Entice people to pull away from God by appealing to their lusts. *But every man is tempted, when he is drawn away of his own lust, and enticed* (James 1:14). John tells us what Satan's toolbox of enticements contains in 1 John 2:16…

a. The lust of the flesh—the strong physical desires of the body, such as food, drink, rest, and sexual pleasure. There is nothing wrong with these desires unless Satan manipulates them and people become deceived by schemes and fall prey to his enticements. Natural desire then becomes sinful.

b. The lust of the eyes—things that appeal to the ego for self-gratification and self-promotion.

c. The pride of life—corrupting the free will God gives man. Satan appeals to man that he can be his own god. The vast majority of Christians cringe at the thought of being independent from God, but Satan is subtler than that. If he can get us to feel we have found a formula to do God's work, then we have already fallen prey to Satan's enticement tool dealing with the pride of life. God's work is performed by people who humbly submit to His Word and His Spirit to fulfill His will on earth, not man-made ideas.

Satan used all these items from his toolbox when it came to Adam and Eve. Genesis 2:9 tells us God made *every* tree that is *pleasant to the sight*, and *good for food.* He told Adam and Eve they could freely eat of every tree except one, the Tree of Knowledge of Good and Evil. Satan came to Eve in the form of the serpent and steered the conversation to *that* tree, stirring up trouble and discontentment. Eve should have been content with a garden full of good things, since *every* tree was pleasant to the sight and good for food. She made a conscience decision to defy God's command not to eat of the Tree of Knowledge, and Satan was there to help facilitate the process:

1. By attempting to corrupt the Word of God. *Ye shall not surely die* (Genesis 3:4–5).

2. And by enticing…

a. The lust of the flesh—*The woman saw that the tree was good for food* (Genesis 3:6a).

b. The lust of the eyes—*It was pleasant to the eyes, and a tree to be desired to make one wise* (Genesis 3:6b).

c. The pride of life—*For God doth know that in the day ye eat thereof, then your eyes shall be opened, and ye shall be as gods, knowing good and evil* (Genesis 3:5).

Satan painted a picture of illusion to Eve, but her *own* lust caused her to defy God. We are only victims of Satan if we choose to be. If we choose to walk with God, He provides provision for man to see through the schemes of "the old serpent," a roadmap around the web of deceit Satan has woven to entangle the human race.

If Eve had wanted to give a truth test to her conversation with the serpent, she could have turned over the rocks and examined carefully. She could have said to the serpent, "I will discuss this conversation with God when Adam and I walk with Him in the cool of the day and will get back to you later." Satan took advantage of her human tendency to take things at face value without asking questions. He drew Eve into his web.

Let's look more at Satan's attempts to corrupt the Word…

Since faith comes by hearing and hearing by the Word of God, as stated in Romans 10:17, Satan desires to corrupt the message.

Recently CBS television network's *60 Minutes* aired a report titled, "Don't Fall Victim to Olive Oil Fraud," which highlighted how fake or adulterated olive oil has become big business for the Mafia to the tune of billions of dollars annually.

60 Minutes producer Guy Campanile described how the knockoff olive oil is deodorized with chemicals and then rebranded as more expensive 100-percent pure Italian extra virgin oil. This scam by organized crime has become known in Italy as "Agromafia."

Paul writes to the Corinthians, concerning a similar attempt to corrupt the Word of God. *For we are not as many, which corrupt the word of God: but as of sincerity, but as of God, in the sight of God speak we in Christ* (II Corinthians 2:17).

The NIV rendition of 2 Corinthians 2:17 states it this way:

> *Unlike so many, we do not peddle the word of God for profit. On the contrary, in Christ we speak before God with sincerity, as those sent from God.*

The Greek word for "corrupt," which Paul used in this passage, is *kapeleuo*, meaning "to retail or adulterate." Paul is saying that he is not watering down or corrupting the word of God because he recognizes that he stands in Christ's presence as he speaks and that it is as if God were looking him in the face.

Sixteenth-century French theologian John Calvin wrote that this word 'corrupt' described "retailers or tavern keepers who were accustomed to adulterating their commodities that they might fetch higher prices."

Calvin described two ways he saw the word of God being corrupted:

1. *"Directly*, when it is mixed with falsehood and lies, so as to be no longer the pure and genuine doctrine of God but falsely commended under that title."

2. *"Indirectly*, when, although retaining its purity, it is turned hither and thither to please men, and is disfigured by unseemly disguises, by way of hunting after favor."

Adulterating the gospel for self gain is fraud. It's committed by greedy, self-seeking people and results in spiritual malnutrition. We're told our fruits and vegetables today do not have the same nutritional value they once did because of unrested soil and overprocessing, which results in illnesses and lack of proper nutrition. The same thing happens to us spiritually when the word we're receiving has been adulterated.

In environments where the word is adulterated, you'll usually find a lack of conviction. Many see conviction as painful, a disruption to comfort, and something to be avoided so as not to offend. This is merchandising the Word of God for the favor of man and self-gain. The preaching of the Word becomes, as pastor and author John MacArthur describes in his sermon, Fool's Gold? Discerning Truth in an Age of Error, "lightweight and without substance, cheap and synthetic, leaving little more than an ephemeral [*short-lived*] impression on the minds of the hearers."

Paul describes to Timothy the people who are caught up in corruption, in II Timothy 3:5, as people having a form of godliness but rejecting—not allowing in—the power that is capable of changing them.

We ask how these things can happen right before our eyes. When looking at olive oil fraud, we can put the deceived people into the two categories below. In Session 2, we'll see that spiritual deception can follow this same pattern:

1. Those who are *not knowledgeable* of the extraordinarily pleasing aroma, rich taste, and luminescent green color of 100-percent pure virgin olive oil from the first pressing of the olive harvest, or

2. Those who *at one time were knowledgeable* of this product many refer to as "the food of the gods." However, because of the vast distractions of today's world, they have become insensitive to the adulteration of the oil—like the deceived frog not realizing it was in water being heated gradually to the boiling point.

As it pertains to those who adulterate God's word, it reveals that they fear men more than God and seek the favor of man over God's favor. The love of self prevails over love for God. It's impossible for the Word of God to be changed by Satan—however, individuals can be deceived when they choose to fall prey to the enemy's schemes to adulterate the Word.

William Booth, founder of the Salvation Army, wrote in Funk & Wagnall's 1902 *Homiletic Review*, Volume 44:

Chief dangers that confront the coming century include the following:

- Religion without the Holy Ghost
- Christianity without Christ
- Forgiveness without repentance
- Salvation without regeneration

- Politics without God
- Heaven without hell

Booth describes an environment where saints slept as Satan took advantage by adulterating the message. *Be sober, be vigilant; because your adversary the devil, as a roaring lion, walketh about, seeking whom he may devour* (I Peter 5:8).

As the writer of Hebrews describes, protection from deception comes by giving the Word of God freedom to do its work in our lives.

For the word of God is quick, and powerful, and sharper than any two edged sword, piercing even to the dividing asunder of soul and spirit, and of the joints and marrow, and is a discerner of the thoughts and intents of the heart.

Neither is there any creature that is not manifest in his sight: but all things are naked and opened unto the eyes of him with whom we have to do (Hebrews 4:12–13).

If we submit ourselves to the Spirit of God, He will guide us into all truth.

Howbeit when he, the Spirit of truth, is come, he will guide you into all truth: for he shall not speak of himself; but whatsoever he shall hear, that shall he speak: and he will shew you things to come (John 16:13).

The children of God hear His voice and follow Him into all truth, led by the Spirit of Truth.

The bar is raised on this generation because of the time in which we live. *For there shall arise false Christs, and false prophets, and shall shew great signs and wonders; insomuch that, if it were possible, they shall deceive the very elect* (Matthew 24:24). Things will be uncovered during these days, things that will shake those who are not grounded in God's Word and not being led by His Spirit. We must seek God as never before.

Finally, my brethren, be strong in the Lord, and in the power of his might. Put on the whole armour of God, that ye may be able to stand against the wiles of the devil (Ephesians 6:10).

Now is *not* the time for weakness or fear—it is a time of strength and courage. Revival is coming to our land. Let us awake. Let us repent for our slumber. Let us crave the Word of God more than our daily meals. Let us pray with intensity. Let us walk in the Spirit daily. *Therefore my dear brothers and sisters, stand firm. Let nothing move you. Always give yourselves fully to the work of the Lord, because you know that your labor in the Lord is not in vain* (1 Corinthians 15:58 NIV).

Reflection on Session One

As you ponder today's session, identify two statements or scriptures that impacted you the most.

_____

_____

_____

Prayerful Consideration

Formulate these statements or scriptures in a prayer of response to God.

_____

_____

_____

Next Steps

What is God asking you to do in response to His voice?

_____

_____

_____

Session Two

The Nine Travelers

When looking at a spiritual walk, every person who has ever lived in this world can be placed into one of two broad categories:

1. Those who *have never* heard the gospel.

2. Those who *have* heard the gospel.

As we examine these in more detail, we are introducing nine user-friendly travelers in Session Two who will help with the process. Some of these travelers walk with Christ daily; others are ordinary sinners; and yet others are what Christ referred to as tares (hypocrites and reprobates). The reader might ask what value this granular level of detail adds to the discussion. The scripture treats hypocrites and reprobates differently than it does ordinary sinners; however, if the enemy can get us to treat them the same, it is an open door for Satan to plant these tares among God's believers for the purpose of disruption and destruction. If we peel back the layers we can gain understanding of what we are dealing with and apply biblical solutions.

All of us can identify with at least one of these travelers, because we see ourselves in them. Here's an important detail:

- Traveler 1 (Category 1) depicts those who *have never* heard the gospel.

- Travelers 2 through 9 (Category 2) depict those who *have* heard the gospel.

Why are there eight travelers depicted in category 2? Each person takes paths based on choices they make. For example, the rich young ruler (depicted by Traveler 6), in Matthew 19:16–30, was on the path of following Christ and seeking to go to the next level of commitment. Christ presented to him what would be required to continue on this path. The sacrifice Christ described was more than the young ruler was willing to make. He chose to walk away rather than deny himself. So he chose to leave the path of walking with Christ in favor of one more comfortable. God gives each person free will to make these choices. However, in full disclosure, in His Word, He also gives the consequences of our choices. What does each path hold for each of the Nine Travelers, and what is the end of each?

Traveler	Description
1	Traveler 1 represents the millions in the world today who have yet to hear the Gospel of Christ.
2	Traveler 2 has heard the gospel, rejected it, and walked away.
3	Traveler 3 has heard the gospel and rejected it but instead of walking away, stayed around.
4	Traveler 4 has heard the gospel and rejected it, is a "tare" as described by Jesus's parable of the wheat and tares in Matthew 13. These are not ordinary sinners; they have wicked and evil hearts.
5	Traveler 5 has heard the gospel, accepted it, and continues to walk with Christ daily, walking in the light of God's Word and in unity with His Spirit, while pursuing spiritual maturity and the fullness of the stature of Christ, void of offense toward God and man (Acts 24:16).
6	Traveler 6 has heard the gospel and initially accepted it but, at some point, stopped allowing the Spirit of God to continue changing him or her into the image of Christ. He or she put up a "Do Not Disturb" sign to the Spirit and walked away. (The rich young ruler fits this category).

7	Traveler 7 has heard the gospel and initially accepted it but, at some point, stopped allowing the Spirit of God to change him or her, putting up a "Do Not Disturb" sign to the Spirit; however, instead of leaving, he or she stays around. In the Old Testament, King David is an example in this category. He sinned against God, but when the prophet Nathan ministered to him, David was very sorrowful and repented. His prayer of repentance is found in Psalm 51.
8	Traveler 8 has heard the gospel and initially accepted it but, at some point, stopped allowing the Spirit of God to change him or her, putting up a "Do Not Disturb" sign to the Spirit and turning into tares—hypocrites and reprobates the enemy plants to bring corruption and destruction to the church, as in Matthew 13:24–30. Scripture refers to these as evil and wicked-hearted, wolves in sheep's clothing. As Paul describes in II Corinthians 11:13, "For such are false apostles, deceitful workers, transforming themselves into the apostles of Christ."
9	Traveler 9 has heard the gospel and initially accepted it, once following Christ closely, now following from afar. The lukewarm people at Laodicea fall into this category. They were given the opportunity to repent or be "spued" out of God's mouth, according to Revelation 3:16.

So what takes place in Traveler 5's life that keeps him or her on the path to spiritual maturity, while others take different paths? It goes back to the choices we make. Numerous scriptures admonish us concerning the importance of God's Word in guiding life choices. *Do not merely listen to the word, and so deceive yourselves. Do what it says* (James 1:22 NIV). The enemy doesn't care how much we read or listen to the Word as long as we don't engage in it. When we conform our actions to the teachings of the Word, that's what makes the difference in whether we are becoming Christlike.

Two people sitting next to each other, as the Word of God is preached or taught, can experience very different results in their lives based on how receptive they are. One can have an open mind and heart, removing all obstacles that prevent the Word from taking root, while the other has a closed heart and distracted mind that prevents the Word from doing its work in his or her life. Jesus addresses this in the parable of the sower:

> *The same day went Jesus out of the house, and sat by the sea side.*
>
> *And great multitudes were gathered together unto him, so that he went into a ship, and sat; and the whole multitude stood on the shore.*
>
> *And he spake many things unto them in parables, saying, Behold, a sower went forth to sow;*
>
> *And when he sowed, some seeds fell by the way side, and the fowls came and devoured them up:*
>
> *Some fell upon stony places, where they had not much earth: and forthwith they sprung up, because they had no deepness of earth:*
>
> *And when the sun was up, they were scorched; and because they had no root, they withered away.*
>
> *And some fell among thorns; and the thorns sprung up, and choked them:*
>
> *But other fell into good ground, and brought forth fruit, some an hundredfold, some sixtyfold, some thirtyfold.*
>
> *Who hath ears to hear, let him hear (Matthew 13:1–9).*

Jesus's parable clearly defines four types of hearers:

- Those with closed minds, reject the Word if it doesn't suit their will and the seeds fall by the wayside. *Yea, they made their hearts as an adamant stone, lest they should hear the law, and the words which the Lord of hosts hath sent in his spirit by the former prophets* (Zechariah 7:12).

- Those who are shallow and have no depth for the Word to take root in their lives. *But the one who hears my words and does not put them into practice is like a man who built a house on the ground without a foundation. The moment the torrent struck that house, it collapsed and its destruction was complete* (Luke 6:49 NIV).

- Those who are distracted with things that have higher priority than God in their lives. These distractions are thorns that choke the effectiveness of the Word.

- Those who receive the Word and engage in it. They conform their actions to the teachings of the Word and, as a result, are living to the fullest.

Each hearer in this parable has a choice of how much priority to place on engaging in the Word of God. Because of our choices, we get different results. For those who choose to continually be present in God's Word, they find the Spirit of God applying His Word to their lives and revealing things that weigh them down or hinder them from moving into the fullness of Christ.

This prompting of the Spirit, which we call "conviction," is our friend. God brings conviction to us because of His love for us. He has a path chosen for each of us that will be the most fruitful, fulfilling life possible, if we choose to walk in it. The conviction we sense alerts us that the Word and the Spirit detect something in our lives that is not of the character of Christ. At that point we make a choice of whether to obey the Word and Spirit, deny self, and continue growing in Christ, or we choose to put up the "Do Not Disturb" sign and refuse to go any further. *Wherefore seeing we also are compassed about with so great a cloud of witnesses, let us lay aside every weight, and the sin which doth so easily beset us, and let us run with patience the race that is set before us* (Hebrews 12:1).

Turning attention back to the account of the rich young ruler, there's an interesting detail in the Scripture (Mark 10:17–22). When the young ruler came to Jesus inquiring about what he needed to do to fully commit his life, the Scripture records a phrase:

Jesus beholding him loved him.

Love was the reason Jesus shared the message with the young man about what it would take to live fully committed. What is our mindset? Would we have celebrated the young ruler just as he was without any challenge from the Word? Do we love people enough to give the message of God's Word as it is, or do we feel the need to alter it for the comfort of the hearers? Sometimes people think that to love someone means we can't say anything that risks offense, so we make people feel comfortable as they are. True love for people creates the desire to be led by the Spirit of God as we minister the Word of God. Only His Spirit can draw someone to Himself.

Love and truth go hand in hand. God only anoints what is His. If we stray from the Spirit of truth as we preach or teach the Word of God, there will be no anointing associated with it. If we pervert the Word by taking liberties to design it the way we want to present it, then it ceases to be God's Word and becomes something man-made that loses the favor of God. Based on the ability of the speaker, the corrupted message might even sound like fine art, persuading shallow hearers. As mentioned in Session One, Paul in II Corinthians 2:17 says he is careful not to corrupt the Word because it's as if he were standing in the presence of God and looking at Him in the face as he shares the Word.

Deception Flag Satan tries to corrupt the meaning of Love.

The beauty of God's plan is that His children know His voice and follow Him. They also know when it isn't His voice. God's children will get this. We can do nothing within ourselves. If we water down or corrupt the Word of God to keep from offending anyone, that's not love. That is greedy, self-seeking, and hunting after man's favor.

Let's resume the discussion of the Travelers.

Deception Flag

Satan deceives some into believing that Traveler 3 and Traveler 7 are the same as Traveler 4 and Traveler 8, respectively. However, scripture treats them very differently. Satan takes every opportunity, while people sleep, to plant his tares in the church for the purpose of destruction.

In an article titled "5 Indicators of an Evil and Wicked Heart," Christian counselor Leslie Vernick describes some of the differences between someone with an evil heart and an ordinary sinner. Evil hearts have no remorse, deceiving without a conscience, and have no fear of God while pretending to be spiritually committed. Vernick goes on to say that evil hearts crave and demand control, that their highest authority is their own self-reference (see Romans 2:8). They reject feedback, real accountability, and make up their own rules to live by, using scripture to their own advantage but ignoring and rejecting passages that might require self-correction and repentance (see Psalms 10, 36:1–4, 50:16–22, 73:6–9; Proverbs 21:24; Jude 8–16).

They delight in sin while still masquerading as someone of noble character. *Who delight in doing wrong and rejoice in the perverseness of evil, whose paths are crooked and who are devious in their ways* (Proverbs 2:14–15 NIV). Vernick states that these want you to believe their horrible actions should have no serious or painful consequences.

But when grace is shown to the wicked, they do not learn righteousness, even in a land of uprightness they go on doing evil and do not regard the majesty of the Lord (Isaiah 26:10 NIV). Vernick points out that the Bible has strong words for those whose actions do not match their talk (see 1 John 3:17–18; Jeremiah 7:8, 10; James 1:22, 26). Daniel 12:10 says the wicked will continue to be wicked.

Jesus was a friend of sinners. Sinners should always be welcome among God's children. As they hear the Word of God and are drawn to Him by His Spirit, it brings conviction of sin and repentance. They find hope and joy, and they start on the road to spiritual maturity. However, Jesus treated tares much differently. Jesus said in His parable, in Matthew 13, that the enemy plants the tares among God's people, that it is done while people are sleeping, for the purpose of disrupting God's people.

Hebrews 5:14 tells us the spiritually mature have their senses trained to discern between good and evil, and this is important because evil disguises itself to look good.

We must guard our hearts so the enemy does not find an opportunity to deceive us. Discernment is the state of being submitted to God, His Word, His Spirit, so we are not deceived by the manipulations of Satan and his system. By walking in the light of God's Word, we see the devices of Satan planted in darkness as a trap for us.

Every way of a man is right in his own eyes: but the Lord pondereth the hearts (Proverbs 21:2).

There are many devices in a man's heart; nevertheless the counsel of the Lord, that shall stand (Proverbs 19:21).

But evil men and seducers shall wax worse and worse, deceiving, and being deceived (2 Timothy 3:13).

Some of the most dangerous traps are the things that seem very innocent on the surface, but if we dig down, we find they are birthed in darkness, manipulated by Satan's system. Satan's network influences the world's ideas, opinions, goals, hopes, and views. If Christians allow their minds to be conformed to Satan's world system, they become drowsy and lulled into sleep.

For when for the time ye ought to be teachers, ye have need that one teach you again which be the first principles of the oracles of God; and are become such as have need of milk, and not of strong meat.

For everyone that useth milk is unskillful in the word of righteousness: for he is a babe.

But strong meat belongeth to them that are of full age, even those who by reason of use have their senses exercised to discern both good and evil (Hebrews 5:12–14).

And that, knowing the time, that now it is high time to awake out of sleep: for now is our salvation nearer than when we believed (Romans 13:11).

But have renounced the hidden things of dishonesty, not walking in craftiness, nor handling the word of God deceitfully; but by manifestation of the truth commending ourselves to every man's conscience in the sight of God (II Corinthians 4:2).

Reflection on Session Two

As you ponder today's session, identify two statements or scriptures that impacted you the most.

_____

_____

_____

Prayerful Consideration

Formulate these statements or scriptures in a prayer of response to God.

_____

_____

_____

Next Steps

What is God asking you to do in response to His voice?

_____

_____

_____

Session Three

The "Do Not Disturb" Community

In this session the reader visits the "Do Not Disturb" community. This group acts religious, but they reject the power that could make them godly. *Wherefore the Lord said, For as much as this people draw near me with their mouth, and with their lips do honour me, but have removed their heart far from me, and their fear toward me is taught by the precept of men* (Isaiah 29:13). These people are directly opposite of those who walk in the Spirit.

Some initially accept the gospel, but later they put up a "Do Not Disturb" sign at the point on their journey where Christ asks something of them they are not willing to give. What starts as a tender heart before God becomes increasingly hardened. Humility turns into a self-centered walk after the flesh.

Many in this condition want to keep the appearance that they are still following Christ. Matthew records the same words as Isaiah:

This people draweth nigh unto me with their mouth, and honoureth me with their lips; but their heart is far from me (Matthew 15:8).

Paul describes these to Timothy as ones who have a form of godliness but do not allow the Spirit to have access to their hearts to do His work:

Having a form of godliness, but denying the power thereof: from such turn away (II Timothy 3:5).

The only way we can continue walking toward spiritual maturity is to allow the Spirit to access us. The Spirit presents the Word of God and prompts us to know what is needed for us to grow in Christ's likeness. If we deny access, we become stagnant in our walk with Christ. Up comes the "Do Not Disturb" sign when some are asked to deny self.

Many churches fall prey to the "Do Not Disturb" deception, as if there is a desire to make people comfortable in their current conditions rather than risk offense by speaking the truth in love. At that point the message changes from God's Word to that of the precepts of man. God will not bless where man chooses to corrupt His Word. Jesus did not change His message to the rich young ruler. He spoke the truth in love, and the young man had a choice to make: to deny self and continue walking with Christ or to turn away. If we corrupt the message by changing it to find favor with man, we offend the Holy Spirit, and without Him we can do nothing.

Where God's Word is corrupted, there's a lack of conviction. In that environment, the favor of man is more important than the favor of God. Committed followers of Christ eventually feel they do not belong where this is occurring. It's of great worth for a Christian to find a community of believers where they love people enough to speak and live the Word of God just as it is, without corruption. In this environment, the Holy Spirit is free to work among the people. As the pure Word is preached, taught, and lived, the Spirit reveals to each one what is needed in their lives to be Christlike. For committed followers of Christ who are willing to deny self and continue following Him, finding this fellowship is priceless.

For those who are willing to follow, Christ leads us all to the same place: spiritual maturity. Humans do not determine what that looks like. It was already determined before the foundations of the world, and it is contained in the Word of God. The Spirit of God, the Spirit of truth, leads us to that place as long as we are willing to go there.

We stay in unity with the Spirit as long as we walk daily with Christ, have a committed heart, deny self, and follow Him no matter the cost. We can be certain it will cost us everything. May we be like Paul: *That I may know him, and the power of his resurrection, and the fellowship of his sufferings, being made conformable unto his death* (Philippians 3:10).

There are joys the human mind cannot even comprehend as we follow Christ to where He wants to lead us. *Instead, be very glad—for these trials make you partners with Christ in his suffering, so that you will have the wonderful joy of seeing his glory when it is revealed to all the world* (1 Peter 4:13 NLT).

We do not want to live in vain. Jesus said in Mark 7:7 (NASB), "But in vain do they worship me, teaching as doctrines the precepts of men." These are people who stopped along the way and put up the "Do Not Disturb" sign. They made their own way and did what seemed right in their own eyes. If we continue following Christ to the destination, we will have to let go of the teachings and commandments of man and hold only to His truth. He will shed the light of His Word on our paths so we can continue walking. Ego has to be sacrificed on the altar of obedience. Having our own way cannot be more important than walking in God's way.

> *Wherefore seeing we also are compassed about with so great a cloud of witnesses, let us lay aside every weight, and the sin which doth so easily beset us, and let us run with patience the race that is set before us,*
>
> *Looking unto Jesus the author and finisher of our faith; who for the joy that was set before him endured the cross, despising the shame, and is set down at the right hand of the throne of God (Hebrews 12:1–2).*

Jesus prayed to the Father concerning His followers:

> *That they all may be one;*
>
> *as thou, Father, art in me, and I in thee,*
>
> *that they also may be one in us:*
>
> *that the world may believe*
>
> *that thou hast sent me.*
>
> *And the glory which thou gavest me*
>
> *I have given them; that they may be one,*
>
> *even as we are one:*
>
> *I in them, and thou in me,*
>
> *that they may be made perfect in one;*
>
> *and that the world may know*
>
> *that thou hast sent me, and hast loved them,*
>
> *as thou hast loved me (John 17:21–23).*

Paul explains further in Ephesians (the italics and bold in the following scripture verses were added by the author) that there's only one path that leads to spiritual maturity—the path where Christ is leading us daily, and our hearts are open to His Word and to His Spirit, without reservation.

There is one *body, and One Spirit,*
even as ye are called in One
hope of your calling;
One Lord, One faith, one baptism,
One God and Father of all, who is above all,
and through all, and in you all (Ephesians 4:4-6).
He that descended is the same also that ascended up far
above all heavens, that he might fill all things
And he gave some, apostles; and some, prophets;
and some, evangelists; and some, pastors and teachers;
For the perfecting of the saints, for the work of the ministry,
for the edifying of the body of Christ:
Till we all come in the unity of the faith, and of the knowledge
of the Son of God, unto a perfect man, unto the measure of the
stature of the fullness of Christ:
That we henceforth be no more children, tossed to
and fro, and carried about with every wind of doctrine, by
the sleight of men, and cunning craftiness whereby they lie in wait
to deceive; But speaking the truth in love, may grow up into him
in all things, which is the head, even Christ:
From whom the whole body fitly joined together
and compacted by that which every joint supplieth,
according to the effectual working in the measure
of every part, making increase of the body unto the edifying
of itself in love (Ephesians 4:10–16).

Reflection on Session Three

As you ponder today's session, identify two statements or scriptures that impacted you the most.

_____

_____

_____

Prayerful Consideration

Formulate these statements or scriptures in a prayer of response to God.

_____

_____

_____

Next Steps

What is God asking you to do in response to His voice?

_____

_____

_____

Session Four

Knowledge-Rich, Discernment-Poor

The title of this section, "Knowledge-Rich, Discernment-Poor," comes from a phrase we hear often today: "Data-Rich." We look for cell phone plans that give us the most data access. Companies pay billions of dollars for access to data that helps in business decisions. However, one of the great challenges for entities today is reflected in this phrase: "Data-Rich, Information-Poor." This describes many entities who have obtained mega-data but have found it doesn't do them any good without the ability to turn the data into usable information for which they can gain understanding.

Paul described to Timothy, in II Timothy 3:7, a people who constantly obtained more knowledge but were not able to reach truth. Satan is not concerned about how much knowledge we gain as long as there is no discernment to allow us to reach full understanding.

The Old Testament prophet Isaiah says it is time to awake!

Awake, awake; put on thy strength, O Zion; put on thy beautiful garments, O Jerusalem, the holy city: for henceforth there shall no more come into thee the uncircumcised and the unclean (Isaiah 52:1).

Wherefore he saith, Awake thou that sleepest, and arise from the dead, and Christ shall give thee light (Ephesians 5:14).

Pioneering surgeon and author Dr. Paul Brand describes in his book, *Fearfully and Wonderfully Made*, the function of white blood cells in our physical bodies:

"More interesting are the white blood cells, the armed forces of the body which guard against invaders. When the attack occurs, an alarm seems to sound. There are fifty billion active white cells in the adult human and a backup force in reserve in the bone marrow. To combat threats, some of the blood's white cells are specifically targeted to one type of invader. These cells spend their lives coursing through the bloodstream, waiting, scouting. When called upon, they hold within them the power to disarm a foreign agent that could cause the destruction of every cell in the body."

If the human immune system is compromised, the body has limited defense against intruders; unless there is divine intervention. The same is true with the defense in the spiritual body; but what causes a weakened immune system in the church? Not ordinary sinners, but tares (hypocrites and reprobates) do.

As we saw with the Nine Travelers, there is a difference between ordinary sinners and tares. Sinners should be welcomed in our midst, where the Spirit of truth anoints preaching and teaching the Word to bring conviction and repentance. They should know they can find help among God's people. However, when hypocrites and reprobates (tares) operate in the body, it is for the purpose of destruction. Conviction wanes where they are allowed to corrupt. Where they are free to work, the church lacks productiveness, regardless of the amount of activity. As tares blend into the body, slumber is perpetuated. *For he that eateth and drinketh unworthily, eateth and drinketh damnation to himself, not discerning the Lord's body. For this cause many are weak and sickly among you, and many sleep* (1 Corinthians 11:29–30). Satan takes the opportunity to place the tares in the body to disrupt, to be a stumbling block, a snare, to bring vexation.

Below are Jesus's words in the parable of the wheat and the tares (degenerate wheat):

> *Another parable put he forth unto them, saying, The kingdom of heaven is likened unto a man which sowed good seed in his field: But while men slept, his enemy came and sowed tares among the wheat, and went his way. But when the blade was sprung up, and brought forth fruit, then appeared the tares also. So the servants of the householder came and said unto him, Sir, didst not thou sow good seed in thy field? from whence then hath it tares? He said unto them, An enemy hath done this. The servants said unto him, Wilt thou then that we go and gather them up? But he said, Nay; lest while ye gather up the tares, ye root up also the wheat with them. Let*

both grow together until the harvest: and in the time of harvest I will say to the reapers, Gather ye together first the tares, and bind them in bundles to burn them: but gather the wheat into my barn.

Then Jesus sent the multitude away and went into the house: and his disciples came unto him, saying, Declare unto us the parable of the tares of the field. He answered and said unto them, He that soweth the good seed is the Son of man; The field is the world; the good seed are the children of the kingdom; but the tares are the children of the wicked one; The enemy that sowed them is the devil; the harvest is the end of the world; and the reapers are the angels. As therefore the tares are gathered and burned in the fire; so shall it be in the end of this world. The Son of man shall send forth his angels, and they shall gather out of his kingdom all things that offend, and them which do iniquity; And shall cast them into a furnace of fire: there shall be wailing and gnashing of teeth. Then shall the righteous shine forth as the sun in the kingdom of their Father. Who hath ears to hear, let him hear (Matthew 13:24–30, 36–43).

Jesus's parable leaves the reader to conclude that if the watchers had been awake, sober, and vigilant, the enemy would not have been able to plant his tares among the children of God. The slumber of the saints created an opportunity for Satan to do his deceptive work. When men are asleep, discernment is absent.

In this passage Jesus describes a field consisting of true saints (the wheat) and imposters (the tares). Since Christ is the gatekeeper of the kingdom, only true saints abide there. *Jesus saith unto him, I am the way, the truth, and the life: no man cometh unto the Father, but by me* (John 14:6).

That is not the case with the church. *Verily I say unto you, Whatsoever ye shall bind on earth shall be bound in heaven: and whatsoever ye shall loose on earth shall be loosed in heaven* (Matthew 18:18). This is quite a responsibility Christ left for His church on earth. But because saints slept and discernment waned, Satan took advantage and planted his tares in the church for the purpose of deception and destruction.

Minister and author John Bevere, in his book, *Good or God,* says, "It's not going to be blatant evil that deceives the elect. It's going to be evil that is masked with good."

The Role of Discernment

Discernment is the ability to decide between truth and error, right and wrong. John MacArthur said, "Discernment is making careful distinctions in our thinking about truth. The ability to think with discernment is synonymous with the ability to think biblically."

> *Prove all things; hold fast that which is good (Thessalonians 5:21–22).*

As believers, discernment is not optional; it's necessary.

> *According as his divine power hath given unto us all things that pertain unto life and godliness, through the knowledge of him that hath called us to glory and virtue: (2 Peter 1:3).*

> *Don't be deceived, my dear brothers and sisters (James 1:16 NIV).*

Paul warned Timothy that some will depart from the faith by falling prey to seducing spirits. Just because they depart from the faith doesn't necessarily mean they leave the environment. If the people of God are asleep, Satan takes the opportunity to use these people undetected in our midst to speak lies and bring corruption.

> *Now the Spirit speaketh expressly, that in the latter times some shall depart from the faith, giving heed to seducing spirits, and doctrines of devils;*

> *Speaking lies in hypocrisy; having their conscience seared with a hot iron (1 Timothy 4:1–2).*

What are the characteristics of those following seducing spirits?

- People who do not endure sound doctrine.
- People who want to go their own way, being taught things that will appeal to their fleshly natures.
- People who follow false teachers.

When people are being seduced, they are not thinking right, even when they think they are. They are being carried away on a wave of their own lusts. They want a god that does what *they* want. They want God to serve them.

Seducing spirits work according to the principles of Satan's network. They work with the logic of man, apart from the Spirit, doing what seems right in their own eyes. They work according to the principle of the devil, independent from God, attempting to be their own gods. They work according to devilish seductions of the flesh.

John told us to try the spirits to be sure they are of God and not of Satan. *Beloved, believe not every spirit, but try the spirits whether they are of God: because many false prophets are gone out into the world* (1 John 4:1).

Discernment is wisdom and insight that go beyond what is seen and heard. God's word is spiritually discerned. To the human mind that isn't led by the Spirit, the things of God are foolishness.

> *The person without the Spirit does not accept the things that come from the Spirit of God but considers them foolishness, and cannot understand them because they are discerned only through the Spirit (1 Corinthians 2:14).*

> *Who is wise? Let them realize these things.*

> *Who is discerning? Let them understand.*

> *The ways of the Lord are right;*

> *the righteous walk in them,*

> *but the rebellious stumble in them (Hosea 14:9 NIV).*

The world is influenced by Satan-fueled belief systems. Some, by their own choices, have become engulfed in these systems that are anti-God. To use the language of John, they have the spirit of Antichrist. The church is not immune to these. These operate among us and try to fill men's minds with notions of self-sufficiency. They feed pride and vanity. They look to gain applause, to serve their own interests, and they worship money. If the church sleeps, Satan plants these among us. We must be awake and alert.

An example from the Old Testament is the defeat of Israel's army at Ai and the sin of Achan. We look in the book of Joshua for a record of what happened. The first six chapters of Joshua record wonderful experiences for Israel, including the victory at Jericho. But starting in Chapter 7, there are surprises as the thrill of victory recorded in the first six chapters is quickly replaced with the agony of defeat. The distance between a great victory and a great defeat can be very short.

After Jericho, the conquest of Ai was essential because it gave Israel control of the main route that ran along the highlands from the north to the central portion of the land. God gave instructions concerning the upcoming battle. The battle confronting Israel was more than a quest for the land. There was a theocratic war raging. Would Israel obey or disobey God? Jesus told us man cannot serve God *and* mammon. This is still the test today. Will we humble ourselves before the Almighty God and obey Him, or will we do things our way?

The test in Ai involved some items placed under a "ban" by God:

a. Everything living must be destroyed.
b. All valuable items, such as silver and gold, were to be dedicated to the treasury.

The disobedience is recorded as such:

> *But the Israelites were unfaithful in regard to the devoted things; Achan son of Karmi, the son of Zimri, the son of Zerah, of the tribe of Judah, took some of them. So the Lord's anger burned against Israel (Joshua 7:1).*

Israel proved unfaithful in the test. The word "unfaithful" here comes from a word that means "underhanded." Achan took some of the items God had placed under the ban, and the anger of the Lord burned against the sons of Israel. The Lord held the whole camp of Israel accountable for the act of one man, withholding His blessing until the matter was corrected. There was sin in the camp, and God would not continue blessing the nation as long as this was so. It doesn't mean this was the only sin and that the rest of the nation was sinless, but this sin was of such a nature—direct disobedience and rebellion—that God used it to teach Israel, and all of humanity, some important lessons.

Achan's behavior illustrates how one or a few who are out of fellowship with God, pursuing their own selfish desires and agendas, can negatively impact the whole. Achan had become a "troubler" to the nation because of his sin. The site of Achan's death and grave was called "The Valley of Achor," Hebrew for "disturbance" or "trouble."

> *Then Joshua, together with all Israel, took Achan son of Zerah, the silver, the robe, the gold bar, his sons and daughters, his cattle, donkeys and sheep, his tent and all that he had, to the Valley of Achor. Joshua*

said, "Why have you brought this trouble on us? The Lord will bring trouble on you today" (Joshua 7:24–25 NIV).

Paul saw this same principle at work in the church concerning sin not judged. He said it contaminated the whole assembly. A little leaven leavens the whole lump of dough.

Your boasting is not good. Don't you know that a little yeast leavens the whole batch of dough? Get rid of the old yeast, so that you may be a new unleavened batch—as you really are. For Christ, our Passover lamb, has been sacrificed (1 Corinthians 5:6–7 NIV).

Paul told the church at Corinth that it was their responsibility to judge within the church.

Therefore let us keep the Festival, not with the old bread leavened with malice and wickedness, but with the unleavened bread of sincerity and truth.

I wrote to you in my letter not to associate with sexually immoral people—not at all meaning the people of this world who are immoral, or the greedy and swindlers, or idolaters. In that case you would have to leave this world. But now I am writing to you that you must not associate with anyone who claims to be a brother or sister but is sexually immoral or greedy, an idolater or slanderer, a drunkard or swindler. Do not even eat with such people.

What business is it of mine to judge those outside the church? Are you not to judge those inside? God will judge those outside. "Expel the wicked person from among you" (1 Corinthians 5:8–13 NIV).

It's interesting to note that in the account with Achan, though one person committed the crime, the whole nation was considered guilty. The nation was responsible for the obedience of every citizen and charged with the punishment of every offender. With this as a backdrop, this passage in Hebrews comes to life:

See to it that no one falls short of the grace of God and that no bitter root grows up to cause trouble and defile many. See that no one is sexually immoral, or is godless like Esau, who for a single meal sold his inheritance rights as the oldest son (Hebrews 12:15–16).

Hiding sin creates trouble.

> *He that covereth his sins shall not prosper: but whoso confesseth and forsaketh them shall have mercy (Proverbs 28:13).*

Nothing escapes the omniscience of God.

> *Do not be deceived: God cannot be mocked. A man reaps what he sows. Whoever sows to please their flesh, from the flesh will reap destruction; whoever sows to please the Spirit, from the Spirit will reap eternal life (Galatians 6:7–8).*

> *But if ye will not do so, behold, ye have sinned against the LORD: and be sure your sin will find you out (Numbers 32:23).*

This verse doesn't just teach us that sin will be discovered, but that the consequences of our sin become active agents in discovering us.

Love in action means we hate evil and embrace good.

> *Love must be sincere. Hate what is evil; cling to what is good (Romans 12:9 NIV).*

If we fall prey to Satan's corrupt definition of love, we break loose from the anchor and become disoriented. We no longer have the ability to discern the things of God. What we once understood becomes darkened.

> *Woe unto them that call evil good, and good evil; that put darkness for light, and light for darkness; that put bitter for sweet, and sweet for bitter (Isaiah 5:20).*

> *Because that, when they knew God, they glorified him not as God, neither were thankful; but became vain in their imaginations, and their foolish heart was darkened (Romans 1:21).*

If we evaluate the defeat at Ai we find distraction and pride were factors that contributed to the failure. The people felt self-confident after recent victories. Joshua was distracted because he was consumed with making plans to continue the move forward. If we do a root cause analysis we see four deadly errors:

1. They remained ignorant of the sin of Achan.
2. They underestimated the strength of the enemy.
3. They overestimated their own strength.

4.   They took the Lord for granted.

If we rush forward with our plans and do not take time with God, we become insensitive to Him. That leads to allowing things around us and in our lives that grieve the Holy Spirit. Grieving the Spirit leaves us defenseless against the enemy because we are operating in our own strength and understanding.

> *And grieve not the holy Spirit of God, whereby ye are sealed unto the day of redemption (Ephesians 4:30).*

The defeat at Ai demoralized the people.

> *And the men of Ai smote of them about thirty and six men: for they chased them from before the gate even unto Shebarim, and smote them in the going down: wherefore the hearts of the people melted, and became as water (Joshua 7:5).*

But rather than examine their own lives as the source of their defeat, they began to doubt the Lord.

> *And Joshua said, "Alas, Sovereign Lord, why did you ever bring this people across the Jordan to deliver us into the hands of the Amorites to destroy us? If only we had been content to stay on the other side of the Jordan (Joshua 7:7 NIV)*

This was one of three questions Joshua asked God as he was spending a whole day on his face. Following are God's assessment of the situation and His instructions to Joshua:

> *The Lord said to Joshua, "Stand up! What are you doing down on your face? Israel has sinned; they have violated my covenant, which I commanded them to keep. They have taken some of the devoted things; they have stolen, they have lied, they have put them with their own possessions. That is why the Israelites cannot stand against their enemies; they turn their backs and run because they have been made liable to destruction. I will not be with you anymore unless you destroy whatever among you is devoted to destruction.*
>
> *"Go, consecrate the people. Tell them, 'Consecrate yourselves in preparation for tomorrow; for this is what the Lord, the God of Israel, says: There are devoted things among you, Israel. You cannot stand against your enemies until you remove them.*

"In the morning, present yourselves tribe by tribe. The tribe the Lord chooses shall come forward clan by clan; the clan the Lord chooses shall come forward family by family; and the family the Lord chooses shall come forward man by man. Whoever is caught with the devoted things shall be destroyed by fire, along with all that belongs to him. He has violated the covenant of the Lord and has done an outrageous thing in Israel!" Joshua 7:10–15).

Because Israel had not dealt with Achan's unconfessed sin, it resulted in weakness and inability to serve and live for the Lord. Why? Because sin grieves and quenches the Spirit. Failure to confront and deal with sin keeps the Lord from prospering our walks.

Achan's confession was the product of discovery rather than an act of repentance or godly sorrow leading to repentance. Confession without repentance or genuine change is hollow, and sometimes confession is too late to stop the discipline.

Achan's sin appears to have grown out of dissatisfaction with his life. Paul instructs us to not be ignorant of Satan's devices. If we are ignorant, that's when Satan gets an advantage on us.

Lest Satan should get an advantage of us: for we are not ignorant of his devices (2 Corinthians 2:11).

This is why it is said:

"Wake up, sleeper,
rise from the dead,
and Christ will shine on you" (Ephesians 5:14).

Let us awake and seek God with all our hearts. We live in an upside-down world, where good is shunned and evil is embraced. Jeremiah told God's people in his prophecies that they lived in the midst of deceit and that's why there was perpetual backsliding.

Thine habitation is in the midst of deceit; through deceit they refuse to know me, saith the Lord (Jeremiah 9:6).

Why then is this people of Jerusalem slidden back by a perpetual backsliding? they hold fast deceit, they refuse to return (Jeremiah 8:5).

Cleanse Us, O God.

> *Who shall ascend into the hill of the LORD? or who shall stand in his holy place?*
>
> *He that hath clean hands, and a pure heart; who hath not lifted up his soul unto vanity, nor sworn deceitfully.*
>
> *He shall receive the blessing from the LORD, and righteousness from the God of his salvation.*
>
> *This is the generation of them that seek him, that seek thy face, O Jacob (Psalm 24:3–6).*
>
> *If my people, which are called by my name, shall humble themselves, and pray, and seek my face, and turn from their wicked ways; then will I hear from heaven, and will forgive their sin, and will heal their land (2 Chronicles 7:14).*

Let us pray the following prayers with our whole hearts:

> *Shew me thy ways, O Lord; teach me thy paths.*
>
> *Lead me in thy truth, and teach me: for thou art the God of my salvation; on thee do I wait all the day (Psalm 25:4–5).*
>
> *O God, thou art my God; early will I seek thee: my soul thirsteth for thee, my flesh longeth for thee in a dry and thirsty land, where no water is;*
>
> *To see thy power and thy glory, so as I have seen thee in the sanctuary.*
>
> *Because thy lovingkindness is better than life, my lips shall praise thee.*
>
> *Thus will I bless thee while I live: I will lift up my hands in thy name.*
>
> *My soul shall be satisfied as with marrow and fatness; and my mouth shall praise thee with joyful lips:*
>
> *When I remember thee upon my bed, and meditate on thee in the night watches.*
>
> *Because thou hast been my help, therefore in the shadow of thy wings will I rejoice.*
>
> *My soul followeth hard after thee: thy right hand upholdeth me (Psalm 63:1–8).*

Paul's prayer for the Philippians was that their love would abound and that they would gain understanding so they would be able to discern.

> *And this I pray, that your love may abound yet more and more in knowledge and in all judgment;*
>
> *That ye may approve things that are excellent; that ye may be sincere and without offence till the day of Christ.*
>
> *Being filled with the fruits of righteousness, which are by Jesus Christ, unto the glory and praise of God (Philippians 1:9–11).*

Godly discernment helps us to distinguish between what is "best" from what is merely "good." James exhorts us to seek the wisdom that comes from above.

> *But the wisdom that is from above is first pure, then peaceable, gentle, and easy to be intreated, full of mercy and good fruits, without partiality, and without hypocrisy (James 3:17).*

In this deceitful world, we must turn over the rocks and examine things. Otherwise, we become very shallow people. Love seeks out truth. Steve Sutherland was quoted in a Charisma News article April 8, 2015, "We want to build a church rather than break a heart. This leaves people confused and deceived because we teach and live a form of Christianity void of repentance…void of truth. Repentance is rarely sought and sin is often excused."

> *This know also, that in the last days perilous times shall come.*
>
> *For men shall be lovers of their own selves, covetous, boasters, proud, blasphemers, disobedient to parents, unthankful, unholy,*
>
> *Without natural affection, trucebreakers, false accusers, incontinent, fierce, despisers of those that are good,*
>
> *Traitors, heady, high-minded, lovers of pleasures more than lovers of God;*
>
> *Having a form of godliness, but denying the power thereof: from such turn away (2 Timothy 3:1–5).*

Peter tells us judgment will start in the house of God.

> *For the time is come that judgment must begin at the house of God: and if it first begin at us, what shall the end be of them that obey not the gospel of God? (1 Peter 4:17).*

The church at Laodicea was lulled into sleep and deceived by the enemy. As recorded below, they saw themselves much differently than what God saw.

> *And unto the angel of the church of the Laodiceans write; These things saith the Amen, the faithful and true witness, the beginning of the creation of God;*
>
> *I know thy works, that thou art neither cold nor hot: I would thou wert cold or hot.*
>
> *So then because thou art lukewarm, and neither cold nor hot, I will spue thee out of my mouth.*
>
> *Because thou sayest, I am rich, and increased with goods, and have need of nothing; and knowest not that thou art wretched, and miserable, and poor, and blind, and naked:*
>
> *I counsel thee to buy of me gold tried in the fire, that thou mayest be rich; and white raiment, that thou mayest be clothed, and that the shame of thy nakedness do not appear; and anoint thine eyes with eyesalve, that thou mayest see.*
>
> *As many as I love, I rebuke and chasten: be zealous therefore, and repent (Revelation 3:14–19).*

The book of Joel parallels much of what we see in our world today. God's people in Joel's day were prosperous but apathetic—they had religion but not relationship.

As in Joel's day, satanic influences destroy hearts and minds. Families have been devoured. Truth has fallen in the streets.

God offered the solution to Joel:

> *Sanctify ye a fast, call a solemn assembly, gather the elders and all the inhabitants of the land into the house of the LORD your God, and cry unto the Lord (Joel 1:14).*
>
> *"Yet even now," declares the Lord,*
>
> *"Return to Me with all your heart,*
>
> *And with fasting, weeping and mourning;*
>
> *And rend your heart and not your garments."V*

Now return to the Lord your God,
For He is gracious and compassionate,
Slow to anger, abounding in lovingkindness
And relenting of evil.
Who knows whether He will not turn and relent
And leave a blessing behind Him,
Even a grain offering and a drink offering
For the Lord your God? (Joel 2:12–14 NASB).

Deception Flag

Satan deceives many into believing God's patience is the same as His approval.

Reflection on Session Four

As you ponder today's session, identify two statements or scriptures that impacted you the most.

_____

_____

_____

Prayerful Consideration

Formulate these statements or scriptures in a prayer of response to God.

_____

_____

_____

Next Steps

What is God asking you to do in response to His voice?

_____

_____

_____

Session Five

Conclusion: A Call to Humility

Having therefore these promises, dearly beloved, let us cleanse ourselves from all filthiness of the flesh and spirit, perfecting holiness in the fear of God (II Corinthians 7:11).

If my people, which are called by my name, shall humble themselves, and pray, and seek my face, and turn from their wicked ways; then will I hear from heaven, and will forgive their sin, and will heal their land (II Chronicles 7:14).

Theocracy is a form of government through which God is the supreme ruler. When Lucifer was an angel in heaven, he couldn't deal with God being supreme. Ever since the war in heaven when Lucifer and his angels were cast out, his plan is to sit on the throne of every man's heart. All of his schemes to deceive man are designed for that purpose. God gives each person a choice as to which master he or she will select to sit on the throne of his or her heart. The history of mankind is a record of this struggle. For those Satan attempts to capture, he paints a beautiful picture of contentment, fulfillment, and independence; but beneath the surface are hopelessness, despair, and unrest.

In Jesus's invitation to discipleship, He shares reality. There is no guile, no deceit, found in His mouth—the direct opposite of Satan. Christ describes the journey just like it is. He invites all weary travelers to join Him for the journey, where we find rest for our souls. He also tells us what is necessary to learn meekness and lowliness from Him.

Take my yoke upon you, and learn of me; for I am meek and lowly in heart: and ye shall find rest unto your souls (Matthew 11:29).

Humility is an attitude of our hearts and minds, making us content to submit to the Father. It requires the "death" of self will. As long as self is alive, it seeks its own desires, which are contrary to God's way. The humble person is not continually concerned with his or her own ways, ideas, and wishes. He or she is not self-willed.

When Paul (formerly Saul) was arrested by the

Spirit on the road to Damascus, he gave the account in Acts. He had been kicking against the will of God.

> We all fell to the ground, and I heard a voice saying to me in Aramaic, "Saul, Saul, why do you persecute me? It is hard for you to kick against the goads" (Acts 26:14 NIV).

But after submitting to Christ and taking up His yoke for the journey, this is Paul's new message:

> Finally, my brethren, rejoice in the Lord. To write the same things to you, to me indeed is not grievous, but for you it is safe.
>
> Beware of dogs, beware of evil workers, beware of the concision.
>
> For we are the circumcision, which worship God in the spirit, and rejoice in Christ Jesus, and have no confidence in the flesh.
>
> Though I might also have confidence in the flesh. If any other man thinketh that he hath whereof he might trust in the flesh, I more:
>
> Circumcised the eighth day, of the stock of Israel, of the tribe of Benjamin, an Hebrew of the Hebrews; as touching the law, a Pharisee;
>
> Concerning zeal, persecuting the church; touching the righteousness which is in the law, blameless.
>
> But what things were gain to me, those I counted loss for Christ.
>
> Yea doubtless, and I count all things but loss for the excellency of the knowledge of Christ Jesus my Lord: for whom I have suffered the loss of all things, and do count them but dung, that I may win Christ,
>
> And be found in him, not having mine own righteousness, which is of the law, but that which is through the faith of Christ, the righteousness which is of God by faith:
>
> That I may know him, and the power of his resurrection, and the fellowship of his sufferings, being made conformable unto his death (Philippians 3:1–10).

Paul gave up all things from his former life, to gain the knowledge of Christ and walk in His righteousness to spiritual maturity. He chose Christ to sit on the throne of his heart, and he never looked back.

Humility makes it possible for us to be obedient to God. Before Jesus became obedient to the cross, He humbled Himself.

And being found in fashion as a man, he humbled himself, and became obedient unto death, even the death of the cross (Philippians 2:8).

Just as the serpent, Satan, attempted to corrupt the Word of God with Eve—and she fell for it—he tries to convince people today that "self" does not have to die. Satan's deceitful message to the world promotes self above all else. Even though Jesus told us that, without Him, we can do nothing, Satan tries to corrupt that message to man by interjecting one of self-sufficiency.

Is God the supreme ruler in our hearts? Let us humble ourselves in the presence of the Almighty God.

But he giveth more grace. Wherefore he saith, God resisteth the proud, but giveth grace unto the humble.

Submit yourselves therefore to God. Resist the devil, and he will flee from you.

Draw nigh to God, and he will draw nigh to you. Cleanse your hands, ye sinners; and purify your hearts, ye double minded.

Be afflicted, and mourn, and weep: let your laughter be turned to mourning, and your joy to heaviness.

Humble yourselves in the sight of the Lord, and he shall lift you up (James 4:6–10).

Wherefore lay apart all filthiness and superfluity of naughtiness, and receive with meekness the engrafted word, which is able to save your souls.

But be ye doers of the word, and not hearers only, deceiving your own selves.

For if any be a hearer of the word, and not a doer, he is like unto a man beholding his natural face in a glass:

For he beholdeth himself, and goeth his way, and straightway forgetteth what manner of man he was.

But whoso looketh into the perfect law of liberty, and continueth therein, he being not a forgetful hearer, but a doer of the work, this man shall be blessed in his deed (James 1:21–25).

God resists the proud but gives grace to the humble. The humble person depends on God—it is the opposite of pride, haughtiness, and self-exaltation.

My sacrifice, O God, is a broken spirit;

a broken and contrite heart

   you, God, will not despise (Psalm 51:17 NIV).

The fear of the Lord is the instruction of wisdom; and before honour is humility (Proverbs 15:33).

Before destruction the heart of man is haughty, and before honour is humility (Proverbs 18:12).

By humility and the fear of the Lord are riches, and honour, and life (Proverbs 22:4).

My sheep hear my voice,

and I know them,

and they follow me:

And I give unto them

eternal life;

and they shall never perish,

neither shall any man

pluck them out of my hand (John 10:27–28).

<u>Reflection on Session Five</u>

As you ponder today's session, identify two statements or scriptures that impacted you the most.

_____

_____

_____

<u>Prayerful Consideration</u>

Formulate these statements or scriptures in a prayer of response to God.

_____

_____

_____

<u>Next Steps</u>

What is God asking you to do in response to His voice?

_____

_____

_____